D1058862

DIALOGUE ON DESTINY

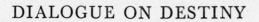

DIALOGUE

ON

DESTINY

BY

George W. Barrett

AND

J. V. Langmead Casserley

GREENWICH . CONNECTICUT . 1955

BT·821
·B24
1955×
·00335710

All Rights Reserved
Printed in Great Britain

Foreword

In Trinity Church, New York City, it is an absolute necessity to present the Christian faith in as many compelling ways as the imagination of its leaders can conceive. All New Yorkers are in a hurry, but Wall Streeters move faster than any of them. The Church has to fish with a big net there. Consequently, a wide program exists at Trinity. It takes place with large congregations in the church itself and reaches an increasing number of organized groups which meet in one of the few parish houses in the world built into a skyscraper. In 1953 more than a million people had their attention caught sufficiently to stop in the mad rush of the financial district's materialistic pursuits to hear the Gospel of Christ preached by a hundred different methods.

One of those methods used for the first time in 1953 was the "dialogue sermon". In a dialogue two razor-sharp minds are needed. Fortunately we had them in two professors from nearby General Theological Seminary: Drs. J. V. Langmead Casserley and George W. Barrett. Since these talks were delivered in Advent, we decided to deal with the great themes of the Last Things: Death, Judgment, Heaven, and Hell. This was surprising enough to people who have grown up in an age when most preaching had avoided these themes like the plague. But it was also a refreshing shock for many to hear somebody talk back in church.

Because this way of preaching was valuable at Trinity, I urged the preachers to publish their dialogues. I hope what they said speaks for itself and inspires others to try this method too.

JOHN HEUSS

Contents

Foreword   5

Preface   9

1 The End of the World   21

2 Death and after Death   41

3 Heaven and Hell   61

4 Kingdom Come   81

Preface

These dialogues are based on four dialogue sermons which we gave together at Trinity Church, New York, on four Sundays of Advent. We are very grateful to the rector, Dr. John Heuss, for giving us an opportunity to introduce his congregation to the method of dialogue preaching and teaching, and perhaps we should add that it was at his suggestion, and with his encouragement, that we arranged these four dialogues in a form suitable for publication.

In arranging the dialogues for publication we transferred them, so to speak, from the setting of the pulpit and the parish church to the more private setting of the rector's office or study. The reader should have in mind the kind of situation which arises when a somewhat puzzled and inquiring layman, honestly seeking the truth, sits down with his parish priest to ask him questions and state his own difficulties. No doubt, there will be many readers of this book who have difficulties of their own quite different from those discussed here, and who are concerned about other aspects of Christian teaching. But we hope the book will encourage such people to do what our honest inquirer does: seek out a wise and understanding Christian clergyman or teacher and lay his doubts and difficulties before that man.

The dialogue method of teaching and preaching, though never used with great frequency at any time in the history of the Church, does in fact represent a very ancient usage and custom. A candidate for the degree of doctor in one of the ancient medieval universities—perhaps we sometimes forget that it was the Christian Church that invented the universities —had to earn the honor by sustaining a thesis before the doctors and professors of the institution. Usually some one member of the existing faculty was entrusted with the task of doing everything possible to refute the young candidate's argument. A somewhat similar technique was employed in the Catholic Church of the Middle Ages—still is employed by the Roman Church—in the proceedings which lead to the canonization of saints. Those who argue in favor of the canonization of saints are opposed by a devil's advocate, *advocatus diaboli*, whose task it is to state all the arguments against canonization. At a later date, some of the Jesuit preachers used a similar technique in church and during missions. One priest proclaimed the gospel or taught the faith while another represented the point of view of the atheist or unbeliever. The central idea was to exhibit to the people the power and the capacity of Christian thought to meet and overcome difficulties and objections.

Where the dialogue method is used today, it is still usual for the interrupter to play the part of the unbeliever or skeptic. For the purpose of the discussion, he usually adopts the attitude of a man hostile to Christianity. In this particular series of dialogues, however—chiefly because they were delivered in place of a sermon during the celebration of the Holy Communion—we thought it better to adopt a different technique. Our interrupter is in no sense hostile to Christianity. He is puzzled and bewildered and very uncertain as to what the teaching of the Christian Church really is. On the whole, we think this is very much the more usual attitude of the large number of people who are outside the Church today. Very few of them are positively hostile, but a great many of them are very much uninformed and exceedingly confused in their thinking about the Christian religion. For that matter, there are a great many people inside the Christian Church who have no clear idea about what the Church's teaching really is about a large number of very important questions. Such people will find it helpful in reading this book to identify themselves as closely as possible with the point of view of the inquiring layman.

After we delivered these dialogues, and as a result of the publicity they received, we were asked several times what were the chief advantages of the dialogue method of presenting and preaching and teaching the faith. We think that this method has at least three decided advantages which should recommend it very strongly to parish clergy who, among other things, are called to be the teachers of their people and are therefore anxious to discover and experiment with what may be to them new methods of carrying out their great educational task.

1. This method has the advantage of expressing the faith in a series of answers to the questions which people frequently ask. Real thinking is very largely the art of answering real questions. Even when a thinker sits in his room working out his problem alone, he usually proceeds by asking himself a series of questions and by facing the difficulties which the answer to his last question seems to suggest. The greatest danger that confronts a preacher and teacher is the answering of questions that are not in fact the ones which the inquirers are asking. The dialogue method is not immune to this danger, but, if used well by people who know what it is to get about in the world and who know how to listen with interest to what other people say to them, it is at least possible to overcome this difficulty to some ex-

tent and present the faith as a series of real answers to real questions.

2. Most people find it easier to listen to two voices than to one. After a time, even the best monologue is likely to have a somewhat soothing effect on the audience. Where the dialogue method is used a different situation arises. Just at the point when the preacher is in danger of sending his congregation to sleep, the new voice chimes in discordantly and the congregation wakes up. We may compare the effect of the sudden *fortissimi* in the slow movement of Haydn's *Surprise Symphony*, "to startle the ladies", as Papa Haydn so engagingly remarked. To startle the ladies is not the only function of the interrupter in the dialogue; we can all see that in certain circumstances startling them might be a rather good thing to do.

3. The dialogue method enables the clergy to collaborate together in the work of teaching their people. So long as one man is alone with his own thoughts and his own conscience, as far as his speaking ministry is concerned, there is always, however devoted he may be to his task, the danger that he will concentrate, above all, on those aspects of the Christian faith which particularly appeal to him and sometimes perhaps even confuse the Christian faith with his own private ideas about things in which he is especially interested. When the dialogue method is used, two men with different points of view and

different personal equations have to get together to decide exactly what is to be said. The result is often a more objective, less purely individualistic, presentation of the faith. That is why we are now publishing these dialogues as a joint effort for which we both take equal responsibility. The dialogues cannot be cut up into "what Dr. Barrett said", and "what Dr. Casserley said". What Dr. Barrett said, he said, very possibly at Dr. Casserley's suggestion, and certainly with Dr. Casserley's consent. Conversely, what Dr. Casserley said may in the first place have been proposed by Dr. Barrett, and was certainly said with his full permission. The dialogue method thus has the advantage of placing at the service of the congregation the experience and knowledge of two Christian minds instead of one. Two for the price of one, as the advertisers say, is certainly a more attractive proposition.

So much for the method. What of the matter? These dialogue sermons were delivered during Advent, and so very appropriately we selected the topic of the so-called "last things": death, which comes at the end of everyman's earthly biography; the kingdom of God, which winds up human history; and the prospects and destiny of man in eternity.

These are not subjects which usually receive any great emphasis in modern pulpit teaching. Our culture, in the present phase of its development, is apt to avoid, almost run away from, the thought of death.

Yet death, other people's and our own, is after all one of the great realities of life, and no genuine faith ever tries to evade reality. Christianity is, as is so often said, a historical religion. For the Bible, it is through the facts of life in history that God has spoken. Hence the spiritual discipline of always resolutely facing the facts is a matter of primary importance in the Christian life. No doubt some, at least, of the factors that we have tried to face in these dialogues will be regarded by many people as "unpleasant", but that only makes the discipline of facing them more salutory. The phrase, "Christian realism", is much closer to the spirit of the gospel than any rather vague and loose talk about Christian ideas.

Perhaps we do not always realize as clearly as we should that one of the duties of the Church and the Christian teacher is to correct the bias and distortion of the prevailing culture pattern. Of course, we all know in general that Christianity must try to influence any particular social pattern from the God-ward side and in a direction that leads God-ward. But that is a pious hope and aim which is not always realized. Very often the prevailing culture pattern and *mores* of the civilization from which the members of the Church are drawn tend, on the contrary, to influence the way in which the gospel is taught and proclaimed.

It is important that the Christian teacher and preacher should always be on guard against this insidious danger. The Christian faith and gospel are neither British nor American nor German nor French, neither Eastern nor Western. It is the universal gospel of God, but although it may and must be proclaimed to many different people in many different languages we must always beware of acclimatizing or domesticating it in the process. It is safe to say that in all places and in all times there will be at least some important elements in the Christian gospel which are locally unfashionable and to many people somewhat unwelcome. We must always be careful not to allow these unfashionable elements in the gospel to drop into the background of our preaching and teaching. In our culture the most important of these unfashionable elements are death, sin, and hell, so that among us today the problem of how best to present the Christian testimony to and interpretation of these realities as persuasively and forcefully as possible is an urgent one for the preacher. On the other hand, there is a very real possibility that this present generation, precisely because we are more familiar with violence than our forefathers and faced with the possibility of total human annihilation undreamed in former times, may be more willing to face the fact of death and more ready to ask questions about what lies beyond it. Ours is a time when the only alternative to contemplating the stark threat of the last *thing* is to dwell upon the hope and the promise of the last *things*.

Lastly, we mention the great delight and pleasure which a collaboration of this kind gives to the collaborators. Having done it once, we two will certainly be on the lookout for an opportunity of "doing it again".

George W. Barrett
and
J. V. Langmead Casserley

1 *THE END OF THE WORLD*

The End of the World

Parish Priest: The New Testament takes us into a world poised on the edge of a precipice. Always throughout the New Testament, whether we have in mind the Gospels in which our Lord's ministry begins with the message, "The kingdom of God is at hand", or whether we turn past the Epistles to the last book of the Bible, the Book of Revelation, always there is this idea of a great startling novelty which is ever at hand.

Many of us, finding these ideas not easy to assimilate, may be inclined to say, "Why not ignore these parts of the New Testament which we find so difficult to understand and confine our attention to those parts of the New Testament which seem more significant to us, more within the compass of our understanding?"

But that is too simple a solution of the problem, so simple, indeed, that it is impossible to carry out. In fact it evades rather than solves the problem. For this sense of being perched on the edge of a precipice, of living life just this side of the coming of the kingdom of God, runs all the way through the New Testament. Almost every passage, if we analyze it carefully enough, seems to be steeped with this sense of wide-eyed expectancy. The theme of the coming of the kingdom lies so profoundly at the heart of the gospel message that no Christian can conceivably ignore it. The plain fact is, indeed, that if we ignore all that the New Testament has to say, so often and so emphatically, about this end of all things, which is always at hand, we will never make any sense of the New Testament message at all.

Inquiring Layman: These remarks are provoking and interesting and I see the point of some of them, but in the main what you say puzzles and in some ways repels me. My first question is perhaps about a rather trivial matter, yet a real one. I am jarred by the very idea of stressing the end of all things at this season of the year. You call this Advent, which certainly must mean that you are anticipating the coming of Jesus Christ into the world and preparing to celebrate His birth at Christmas. Indeed, almost everyone in his own way is caught up in preparing for Christmas. I enjoyed seeing the Santa Claus parade on television the other day, and I loved a clever ad in the newspaper which showed Santa Claus finishing off a Thanksgiving turkey and saying, "Now, let's go." Yes, let's go! Decorations are going up on the streets and in department-store windows. The stores are becoming crowded. We are buying presents and will soon be sending cards to our friends. Already, the beautiful Christmas carols are being sung. Why, I heard one in the railroad station the other day, and it gave me a wonderful feeling. I thought how fundamentally Christian Americans are, and no doubt this could be paralleled with Christmas customs in other countries.

This is a time when we think of more than Christmas trees and decorations. It is the season of the year when we try to practice the Christlike spirit; we are kinder to others. We look for ways to make our loved ones happy. We seek to alleviate misery and hunger. We endeavor to mitigate the cruelty, the fear, and the meanness in the world. We try harder to keep the golden rule. We dream of peace on earth and dare to hope for it more confidently. All this we relate to the Christ Child, who grew up and taught us to love one another.

Now, the very Church that claims His name spoils this wonderful spirit by proclaiming negative ideas about the future. I remember a friend of mine who criticized the Christmas decorations in her town. She enjoyed the lights that hung on some trees but objected because there was a large cross in the middle of the trees in the center of the parkway. It was the Christmas after Pearl Harbor. She very truly said, "Why, that cross suggests Easter and all its sadness. We ought to be happy at this season." I am inclined to agree with her and to feel the same way about this emphasis of yours on the end of all things when we are preparing to celebrate the birthday of Christ. Is not this a highly inappropriate method of getting ready for Christmas?

Parish Priest: Well, it might seem to be so, particularly at first sight, when, as so easily happens, our ideas of Christmas are based much more on the advertisements in the newspapers, which we read every day, than on the New Testament, which very likely we read seldom or not at all. While the Santa Claus of the advertisement you mentioned indeed says, "Now, let's go", the real question which I would like to ask is this, "Yes, but *where* are we going?" I imagine that the Santa Claus of the advertisement means, "Now let's go to the department stores and spend as much money as we have," or even, I rather suspect, more than we have. Only yesterday morning I had a circular from a firm whose business it is to lend money, saying, "Christmas is a very expensive time. We shall be delighted to let you have a loan of $500.00 which you can repay in [what they call] sensible monthly installments." It did not, of course, say how "sensible" the monthly installments were to be.

But such a conception of Christmas is in many ways foreign to the New Testament. The Advent season prepares for the commemoration of the coming of Christ and for the coming of the kingdom of God at the end of all things, not merely at the same time, but with the same heart and with the same mood. "Now, let's go", it tells us, "let's go to the kingdom". The very idea of Christmas proclaims that the coming of the King into the world is our guarantee of the ultimate coming of the kingdom. Because God has given us the King, we are more confident that He who gave us the King will not deny us the kingdom. "Fear not, little flock; for it is your Father's good pleasure to give you the kingdom." And the Father's will to give us the King at the first Christmas is the guarantee of the Father's will to give us the kingdom also, as and when He wills to accomplish the purpose of all things.

There is also a deeper connection between the coming of Christ at Christmas and the idea of the end of all things. After all, as we Christians understand it, Christ is the end of all things. He is the King in the kingdom. He is the Judge. He is the ultimate meaning and purpose of human existence. Through Him and in Him we exist as Christians, and for the sake of the purpose which He wills, and came to the earth to accomplish, we live. When we think of the coming of Christ into the world, we think of the end of all things because Christ is the end of all things. Indeed, when we think of Christ coming into the world, we think also of our own personal end as far as this world is concerned.

Christmas is indeed a happy festival, but not happy in quite the usual way. Christ did not come into the world to live a long, happy, and prosperous life. On the contrary, He came into the world to minister, to suffer, and to die; to minister and suffer that we like Him might suffer and minister, and to die that we might live. Our Christmas rejoicing cannot ignore the kind of life to which the birth at Bethlehem was a prelude. The coming of Christ into the world is not simply the birth of an ordinary baby, nor simply the beginning of an ordinary human life. It is the coming into the world of our King, our Judge, He in whom our destiny under God is to be accomplished so that to know the Christ who was born on the first Christmas Day is, in a very profound sense, to know what the end of all things really is.

Inquiring Layman: I agree that we naturally read the significance of a man's career back in his early life and feel that His ultimate destiny was apparent even when He was born, but I can still see no relation between such a statement and what the New Testament obviously means by the end of all things. Certainly, you have in the New Testament the anticipation of an event that the first Christians were sure would take place very soon. Thus, we read in the Epistle to the Romans, "The night is far spent, the day is at hand." When Paul wrote to the Corinthians about death and the resurrection, he said, "We shall not all sleep, but we shall all be changed, in a moment, in the twinkling of an eye . . . for the trumpet shall sound, and the dead shall be raised incorruptible, and we shall be changed." And in writing to the Thessalonians, he was even more explicit, "The Lord himself shall descend from heaven with a shout . . . and the dead in Christ shall rise first: then we which are alive . . . shall be caught up together with them in the clouds, to meet the Lord in the air."

Certainly Paul, at least during the earlier period of his ministry expected that in his own lifetime Christ would come back to end this world and establish a new age. Much of his teaching is based on this assumption. For example, when he writes about marriage he seems to suggest that to be married is permissible but hardly worthwhile when there is so much trouble and so much to do and when the world will probably end the day after tomorrow anyway. And Christ Himself says, "Verily, I say unto you this generation shall not pass away, till all be fulfilled." I wonder if the uncompromising demands He makes about forsaking all and following Him, and being perfect as our Heavenly Father is perfect, are not really based on the idea that the end of all things is at hand and the kingdom of God, in its fullness, about to be established? And the last

27

book of the New Testament begins, "The Revelation of Jesus Christ, which God gave unto him, to shew ... things which must shortly come to pass. ..." At the very end of that book we find the words, "Surely I come quickly."

But He did not come quickly. The Lord did not descend from heaven with a shout. Paul died. Generation after generation, century after century, came and went, and no generation and no century brought the end of all things. Surely we must agree that the early Christians were mistaken in their belief in a speedily approaching end of the world. The explanation for their mistake is really quite simple. They were men of their time and they shared the superstitions of their age. The idea of the end of all things was based upon an erroneous notion, very common in the first century but impossible for us in the twentieth.

Parish Priest: I think we shall have to agree that the minds of the writers of the New Testament were confused about this subject, just as ours are today, for that matter, after two thousand years of careful critical study and reflection. But an idea is not necessarily untrue because we do not understand it properly. It would appear, if we examine the New Testament carefully, that the different passages which deal with the theme of the end of all things refer to different events. Sometimes the reference is to the destruction of Jerusalem, which, of course, was very close at hand. It came about in A.D. 70, in the lifetime of many who had known and listened to Jesus. Sometimes the passages seem to refer to the Resurrection of Christ and to the great outpouring of the Holy Spirit upon the Early Church. The writers of the New Testament documents were men convinced that they had already seen the powers of God let loose. The glory of God was among them and they felt its influence. Within a single generation they saw a Church, which to begin with looked as if it were no more than a weak, persecuted, tiny Jewish sect, leap from Jerusalem to Asia Minor, from Asia Minor to Macedonia and to Greece, and thence to Cyprus, to Egpyt, to Rome, and probably to Spain and the south of France. In their eyes this sudden expansion, which they attributed to the power and inspiration of the Holy Spirit, was a miraculous event, and it is small wonder that they thought so. From their point of view, the kingdom of God had come in a real sense already. Indeed, Jesus Himself several times spoke as though the kingdom of God had already come in His own person and existed in His presence. Thus He can say, "If I by the finger of God cast out devils, no doubt the kingdom of God has come upon you."

But there are still other passages which refer to some "one, far-off, divine event to which the whole creation moves". And of this our Lord warns us that it is not for us to know the times or the seasons. It may well be that the minds of the New Testament writers were confused by these contrasting yet related strands in the teaching of Christ, but this should not make such passages meaningless for us. No, I should still say, for example, that the author of the First Epistle of John was quite right and said something permanently important for all generations of Christians when he told us, "Little children, it is the last time." This is indeed the last time. It is the last time because it is the time in which men can know the last thing.

As I said before, Christ is the last thing; He is the end of all things. We too live, like every generation since New Testament times, in the year, the century, the age in which men, through their Christian faith, can know the end of all things, the Christ. Notice how we arrange our Christian calendar. We say that there were the years B.C., before Christ, and then the years A.D., which does not mean the years after Christ. A.D., Anno Domini, means "in the year of our Lord". These are the years which belong to Christ, the years which lie beneath the judgment of Christ, the years which hope in Christ, pray in Christ, worship in Christ, and aspire in Christ. These are the last times, because they are the times which belong to the last thing, the times in which men know their destiny and know what that consummation is toward which they are moving. The last time need not be a short time; it can still be a very long time and yet be the last time, the time in which we live under the shadow of the judgment and wait and watch for the kingdom.

Inquiring Layman: But I am still bothered about the word "last" and the expression "the end of all things". For today we think in terms of beginnings and progress rather than in terms of endings, which imply finality and which at least hint of decay and defeat. We modern men characteristically believe in progress. This earth is very young, as planets go. Man has been on the earth but a tiny fraction of the life span of this planet. It has not been really very long since the first man had that spark of insight or understanding or conscience that marked him off from the beast. It was only yesterday that he climbed down from the trees. It was only dawn today when he emerged from caves. And in this short time how much he has achieved: the taming of fire, the domestication of animals, the fashioning of tools, and now the harnessing of the source of energy itself! Think of the creation of culture, of civilization, with its law and government, the fine arts, and medicine. Think of the slow evolution of individual freedom and regard for human rights. Think of the marvelous progress of the last two centuries in lifting the burden of drudgery from the backs of so many who labor.

Of course, I am not naïve about this. Not for a minute do I maintain that progress is automatic or that there have not been terrible retrogressions. I do not overlook the ghastly tragedies of the twentieth century nor the deadly threats that now hang over the world. But still I cannot help being optimistic. Somehow I feel we shall solve our worst problems and find a way to bring peace on earth, and once that is done we shall enter an age of plenty and happiness never before known to man.

I look at the Bible and see this hope expressed centuries ago. "The earth shall be full of the knowledge of the Lord, as the waters cover the sea." We pray, "Thy kingdom come". In a very real sense, I hope that the kingdom of God will come upon this earth. At least I should like to believe that. But this is all the more reason why I cannot abide this negative emphasis which threatens to destroy the basis of our faith in man's progress.

Parish Priest: All this certainly raises some very important questions. I will begin by pointing out that even if we listen to the voice of our own science, then, as far as we can tell, there will indeed be an end of all things, or at least an end of organic life on earth. It may be a long time ahead, but nevertheless it will come. So actually there can be no assurance, so far as we know, of man's continual progress. It would appear to have its natural and inevitable term.

I am inclined to question the whole idea of progress from the Christian point of view. It sounds very optimistic as you express it, but when we examine what it really means, we discover that the Christian can have nothing to do with it, at all events in its conventional forms. In the first place, progress is much more concerned about the human race than about individual human beings. The concept of progress reminds me of the attitude of a man engaged in breeding prize-winning cows or pedigree dogs. He is not bothering about this particular cow or dog but about his great-great-great-grandchild, which he hopes will be a much finer cow, a much finer dog. Progress is often indifferent to the human beings who now exist because of its dream about the wonderful human beings who will be in the future. When these wonderful people come in the future, if they do come, then the progressive mind will be concerned not about them but about the still more wonderful beings to be born at an even later stage. As in *Alice in Wonderland*, there is always jam tomorrow, never jam today. The progressive mind seldom cares about human beings as such.

We Christians are much more concerned about the human beings that are alive and with us now, and about their hope of achieving their destiny with God in His eternal kingdom, than about some purely hypothetical wonders and splendors which may appear upon this earth in ten generations' time. We care more about human beings than about the human race. Human beings are eternal realities. The human race is a biological conception. We are talking about the end in this concrete sense: the destiny of each individual man and woman. Progress, in the more abstract sense, may possibly be a reality although I venture to think that progress in this sense has been progress in the intensity and the horror of the conflict between good and evil. As centuries pile upon centuries, this conflict, so far as we can see, becomes ever more intense, ever more destructive, ever more terrible. The potentialities for good seem greater and the potentialities for evil more tragic, and so far as we are talking about the course of events in history, I see no reason to suppose that that will cease to be so at any imaginable future time.

However, it is more important to notice that the word "end" means two things. The end can mean the point at which we leave off and cease to be, but, more usually in ancient literature and in the New Testament, the end means the moment at which we achieve our destiny, the moment at which finally some great consummation comes about which makes sense of everything that led up to it. The end of the play, the great climax, is not the point at which the play stops; it is the point at which the meaning of the play becomes plain. Now, this is what we mean by the end of all things. We do not mean that all things are suddenly terminated. We mean the moment at which the destiny of all things is achieved, and the meaning of all things revealed, in the great event to which all things move. So the phrase, "the end of man" or "the end of all things" in the New Testament, does not mean the point in time at which man ceases to be, but rather the point in time at which man begins to be what he was always meant to be—in the kingdom of God.

Inquiring Layman: I must say that your answers, while convincing in some ways, still leave rather serious questions in my mind. If the end in the New Testament does not really mean a point in time, how are you going to rationalize the use of the many statements in the New Testament writers, as well as in the Church's liturgy and worship, which imply that the end certainly is a point in time?

Do you mean what you say when you affirm in the Creed, "He shall come again, with glory, to judge both the quick and the dead; Whose kingdom shall have no end"? Then there is the daily Collect of the Advent season containing the words, "In the last day, when he shall come again in his glorious majesty to judge both the quick and the dead. . . ." We sing such hymns as:

> Lo! he comes with clouds descending,
> Once for our salvation slain . . .
>
> or
>
> Up, watch in expectation!
> At midnight comes the cry.

What are we to make of the parables that command watching: such as the parable of the Wise and Foolish Virgins and the parable of the Talents? Then there is the parable of the Judgment, when the Son of Man comes in His glory and all nations are gathered before Him.

And at the Holy Communion we are repeatedly reminded of Paul's statement that in this act the Church shows forth the death of her Lord, "until his coming again".

What do these expressions mean to us today?

Parish Priest: Here I think we must face the very fundamental fact that the Christian faith and the Christian Church does use poetical language. The Christian Church all through her history has been a great poet. One of our difficulties today is that so many of us are out of the habit of reading poetry. We should understand the Bible better and the Prayer Book better and take part in the Church's services more creatively if we read poetry more often, because then we would be more accustomed to poetic language. There are many things that can only be said poetically. There are some things that can be said in literal language, such as, "It is raining today" or "Mr. Eisenhower is President of the United States". There are other things described in abstract speech, such as the things we read about in textbooks of science or philosophy or mathematics where we are discussing not concrete realities but abstract ideas. For example, "Parallel lines will not meet even though produced to infinity."

But there are other things which can only be described in poetical speech, things which we dimly discern, but which we know to be as real as the things which we can see clearly and describe precisely. They are not just ideas nor just abstractions. So what do we do? We say they are like something else; we use imaginative poetical language to bring them to light. This is true of the young man in love. If he just gives a literal description of his beloved, we will not see her as he sees her. But if he tells us that his love is like a red, red, rose, which is not literally true, we understand much better how he sees her than if he gave an exact description of eyes, nose, her mouth. The same rule applies in religious communication. Here we are dealing with great promises of God, with great and profound religious insights. To believe in them is part of our faith, but we cannot describe them in literal language, and so we use the great poetical images of "coming again in the clouds of glory . . . the end of the world . . . the inauguration of the Kingdom of God . . . the everlasting worship of the saints before the throne of God in heaven", and so on. Now that is poetical language, and we must receive and use it as poetry. But we must not make the mistake of supposing that, because these particular strands in the rich and tangled skein of New Testament teaching are all expressed in the language of poetry, they are therefore unimportant.

From the beginning the Christian life is always a

life lived in the sure and confident expectation of the coming of the kingdom of God. Indeed, it is a life lived in the strength and inspiration of the belief that in a very real and deep sense the kingdom of God has come already. God has given us our King, and surely in His own good time He will not deny us the kingdom. It is quite impossible, for example, to understand and enter into the meaning of Christian worship unless we share the belief that in our Christian worship—above all in the Eucharist—the kingdom of God really comes and we are gathered into it by our worship and feel and know ourselves to be its citizens. In the Eucharist, at the peak moment of consecration and communion, the worshiper adoringly proclaims and confesses that the Lord Christ has come to reign among His people and that in worshiping Him and receiving His gift of Himself— for the Lord Christ never gives us anything less than Himself—we are really aware of His presence among us as a King in His own kingdom.

2 DEATH AND AFTER DEATH

Death and after Death

Parish Priest: In our last conversation we discussed the statement in the New Testament, "The end of all things is at hand", and also in what sense this statement can still be regarded as true. We said that humanity lives always in the shadow of the end of all things, and that this end is really the coming of the kingdom of God and of His Son Jesus Christ.

Of course, we must never forget that the "end of all things" has an inescapable personal meaning for every man and woman in this world. Everyone dies. Death constantly stalks the earth, and we never know when it will strike us and those whom we love. I suppose that to every man there comes a time when he realizes, "I won't be living on this earth forever. Why, a good half of my life has gone by already, and what have I to show for it?" Much more frequently, the loss of others, especially those whom we love, shocks us into an awareness of the final irreversible, ruthless character of death. Our parents, to whom we owe our lives and upon whom we have never completely ceased depending, die and we have a sense of desertion, a feeling of standing alone—yes, a sense of the end of all things, or at least the end for us of some of the things most familiar and precious. A woman loses her husband and her world ends, a world that meant support, security, and love. Her whole way of life is over. She must courageously create a new life from the fragments that remain. A child, to whom a devoted father and mother gave all the care, the affection, and the wisdom of which they were capable, is killed in a moment, and a large part of that family's world dies with the child.

During World World II an army chaplain came to address a Woman's Auxiliary in the parish of which I was rector. He said, "I am doing exactly the same thing that the Church is always supposed to be doing—preparing men to die."

Before him sat women whose sons were at that moment fighting in Europe or the South Pacific. I saw them wince; in fact, I winced myself. We winced, and not only we. Our whole culture winces at death, winces so much that we try to ignore death. Our funeral customs—indeed our very vocabulary concerning death—seem calculated to sidestep this event. People do not die any longer, they "pass away". A famous cemetery advertises underground crypts so that the loved ones may have the combined advantages of burial in the ground and entombment in a mausoleum. Paul Tillich has written, "The dead are not allowed to show that they are dead. They are transformed into a life mask of the living." All these pathetic masks and childish disguises cannot hide the realities, nor can the Christian Church minister to mankind's deepest needs nor convincingly proclaim the gospel if she fails first to look at the truth. Death is the final, inevitable fact that, sooner or later, everyone must face.

Inquiring Layman: Well, I must say, we seem to be in a gloomy mood today. No doubt what you say is correct enough, but it is not helpful to suffering human beings. You say we must all face death sooner or later. I think you are really asking us to face it sooner rather than later. The real question is whether this is a healthy or necessary thing to do. Of course, we all know perfectly well that sooner or later we must die; but the way of civilization, at all events in recent years (and, if we look back to the way in which they used to look after the dead in ancient Egypt, possibly in early years too), seems to be to try to hide what we might call the darker and gloomier facts of life.

The thing that concerns us is not really death; the

thing that concerns us is life. The best way of getting on with life and ignoring death, I think (and I suggest this to you so that you may agree), is to invent a technique which conceals something of the horror and the terror and the finality of death from the eyes of the living. And so it is, I believe, that we invent a special technique for dealing with the dead and of speaking about the dead to save our minds from being worried and bothered by the thought of death while we are engaged in the tasks of life. I would say that certainly our modern civilized way of dealing with death is really a way of humanizing death so that we can learn to live with death more comfortably.

Parish Priest: It may look that way superficially, but it is never a good thing to refuse to face reality. Of course, it may seem comfortable to ignore unpleasant or painful facts, and indeed, it may be comfortable in the short run. The inhabitants of Pompeii felt secure before Vesuvius erupted. You can feel quite secure in a shoddily built house until the earth begins to shake. Many reveled in wealth and luxury before the stock market crashed and the worldwide depression began in 1929. Many of us rejoiced when the Munich agreement seemed to guarantee "peace in our time".

But one of the sure findings of psychology is that reality cannot be permanently ignored. When we have a devastating experience of fear or pain, or loneliness or rejection, it may be so bitter that we try to forget it. We push it out of our conscious mind, but will not be rid of it. Deep down it festers and grows until it arises to plague us in strange, unrecognized ways. In fact, the only way in which we can be released from its grip is to bring it to the surface and face it. Once so recognized, it can be conquered and its power destroyed.

So we cannot deal with the problem of death until death is frankly recognized for what it is. If we try to disguise it, to push it aside, or to shrug it off in a callous manner, it attacks us, from its ambush in the unconscious, in bitter, unrealized, and devastating ways. Death, in short, must be recognized for what it is—an enemy with tragic power and an enemy who in this world always wins. Death is an adversary who wounds before it kills. Men often die after lingering weakness or in great pain or long after their personalities have been destroyed by senility.

Man dies with guilt on his soul. Paul says, "The sting of death   sin." You feel the sting of death when you realize: 1e missed opportunities, the selfish willfulness, : he empty futility in the best of us. Although we try to hide these facts in our eulogies of the dead and in our appreciation of their genuine virtues, we know that no man leaves this world without the stain of sin upon his soul. Furthermore, we know that no achievement in this world, no earthly adjustment, can produce complete happiness or fulfillment, that underneath the most satisfactory appearances lie a hunger and a restlessness that nothing on earth can satisfy. In the final analysis, then, death is a sheer tragedy.

Inquiring Layman: Of course, I am all in favor of facing the facts when I am really convinced that, if we do face the facts, we can do something about the facts. The difficulty I feel—and I imagine many men would agree with me, including many of the sages of antiquity—is that even if we do face the fact of death, this particular fact is to us so dark, mysterious, and inscrutable that we cannot possibly do anything about it. I remember reading somewhere that Epicurus once remarked that we have nothing to fear in death because there is no life after death and so there will be no judgment after death upon the way in which we have lived this side of death. We cannot be sure, of course, that Epicurus is right. Perhaps there is life after death. As Shakespeare says, many men in trouble and difficulty would "their own quietus make with a bare bodkin", but that "the fear of something after death" gives them pause. Well, we just do not know. It may be that death is the mere end, in which case at least there is nothing to be afraid of. But it may well be—it is just possible —that death is the prelude to something else, something else which includes judgment and many other unknown things on the verge of which we tremble. We just don't know what death is. What is the good of facing a fact if the fact remains unknown even when we face it? It is like raising questions which nobody knows how to answer. It is a waste of time. The best thing to do with questions that we cannot answer is just not to ask them.

Parish Priest: Now, if I were as certain as you seem to be that we cannot answer them, I would agree. But the wonderful truth is that we can answer them. God has given us the answer. The Christian faith affirms that God grants us eternal life, because He loves and cares about us, because He has created us for loving fellowship with Himself. Our fellowship with God begins, or can begin, in this world. Certainly, it is impossible to believe that God would allow death to put an end to lives that He has made for such eternal companionship with Himself.

When Jesus was asked about life beyond death, He answered, "God is not the God of the dead but of the living, for all live unto Him." Here is all the certainty we need. I fully agree with you that many philosophers of the past and present have denied the reality of life after death. I would go further. I find no evidence in psychical research for the survival of the soul or communication with the departed. In fact, our religion has usually taken a very disapproving view of any attempt to communicate with the departed.

Faith in the love and goodness of God is the only unassailable answer to the problem of death. It is a matter of trusting our Lord's character, authority, and assurance. Granted that we cannot prove the reality of eternal life in the same way that we can prove two times two is four; yet we still assert it unqualifiedly as a venture of faith, and we know that only such faith gives life in this world sense and meaning. Because we believe and trust in God the Father Almighty, because we believe in Jesus Christ, His Son our Lord, therefore we believe in the life everlasting.

Inquiring Layman: That is all very interesting and I am glad to hear you say that when you are teaching the life everlasting, you are not teaching in the Christian Church anything that in any way resembles the ridiculous superstitions of many of the spiritualists and occultists. I am relieved to have that distinction made clear. But I still want to ask you to consider this question: Have we possibly made a mistake in thinking in terms of personal immortality? Isn't it true, if you look at the animal world, that nature is always careful of the type, as Alfred Tennyson says, but indifferent to the individual. Thus, crabs come and crabs go, but what goes on through the centuries is just crabs. Now, may it not be true that even with human beings we have made a mistake, that what really lives on and survives for generation after generation is not this or that human being but the human race itself, so that a man has real immortality, as the great English novelist, H. G. Wells, used to teach, not in himself but in his children and his children's children and their children? I want you to consider whether that is not really a profounder and deeper conception of immortality. I live on, so to speak, in the creative good that I have been able to do and to contribute to the future. One is reminded of Walter Savage Landor's poem in which he says:

> I have warmed both hands at the fire of life;
> It fades and I am ready to depart.

What would you say to me were I to ask you something like this: "Look here, I have lived my life, I have had my chance to make my contribution to the lives of those who are going to come after me. What have I got to complain about now?"

Parish Priest: I think you would have several things to complain about. In the first place, any such notion involves an absolutely monstrous idea of the character of God. It means that God is like a craftsman who makes fine tools to accomplish his purpose but that whenever he is through with the tools he callously discards them. It means that God is using us like so many tools for some purpose in which we have no real share, that He throws us aside when our usefulness to Him is over. Why, that would be as vicious a practice as for society to cast aside elderly workers with no responsibility for them in their old age. It has been suggested that a view like yours implies that the men and the women living today, as well as the people of all past generations, are a kind of raw material for a Christless utopia of the future.

But God is not like the sort of humanitarian who cares only for the race. He is a Father who infinitely loves each one of His children, no matter at what period of history they happen to live on this earth. In fact, it was not until the Hebrew people came to believe that God loved them as individuals, and not simply as a nation or a tribe, that they also came to believe in eternal life.

Not only is the doctrine of the immortality of the race a slander upon the character of God; it is also utterly unrealistic when it holds out the hope of living on in the lives of our children. Shakespeare saw more truly than that when he said, "The evil that men do lives after them; the good is oft interred with their bones." Would not the best thing that could happen to many, perhaps most, of our contributions to life be to have them forgotten altogether?

Further, it is possible that man may not have too long a time left on this earth. We have developed the means to fulfill the words of the Second Epistle of Peter, "The day of the Lord will come like a thief, and then the heavens will pass away with a loud noise, and the elements will be dissolved in fire, and the earth and the works upon it will be burned up." That sounds more like the twentieth century than the first. And even if this catastrophe be avoided, we still know, as we have already observed, that this earth will ultimately be unable to sustain life. The earthly life of the human race must come to an end just as much as the earthly life of each individual human being.

Inquiring Layman: Yes, but please consider this. Really, you know, this suggestion of human beings just living on and on forever is a very horrible and intimidating one. You may think you are giving us comfort when you say this, but I am sure to the more thoughtful of us you are giving nothing of the kind. Now, we do find, in some of the old mythologies, stories about men who could not die. There was Tithonus in the old Greek mythology. Then there are the stories of the Wandering Jew and the Flying Dutchman. They, too, could not die. Now, in all these stories, the inability to die is represented as a punishment from God or the gods, and the ability to die as a blessing which all these men desperately desire. They wander over the face of the earth looking for some means which will enable them to die and get them out of the misery of just going on and on and on forever throughout the years without end.

Now, I believe there is a very profound human insight in these stories. They say that just going on forever is not a happy privilege but a miserable fate. I must say I agree. I myself find the idea of just going on and on as I am now really rather horrifying.

Parish Priest: You are certainly right about that.

Who would want to go on living just as he is today, with the same hopes, the same fears, the same jealousies, and the same sins? Who would want to go on living forever unless he were to attain an entirely different kind of life? Who would want eternal life unless it were life with God? A rather famous philosopher once examined this problem and came to the conclusion that he had proved two things: the first was that there is no God; the second, that the soul is immortal. Well, the poor man had proved himself into hell, for what is hell but eternal life without God? This is exactly why the ancient pagan doctrines of immortality are such tragic ones. In them, when a man dies, his soul goes on in some sort of shadowy existence in a land of darkness and unreality. The pagan doctrine of the immortality of the soul has been described as an existence where one is barely aware of not being alive. He is a shade. Even in the familiar ghost sorties, the ghost is usually pictured as desperately unhappy.

But Christians, on the contrary, believe that eternal life is a new, risen life, life in the joy of the Risen Christ. One of the principal commands of the Risen Lord to His disciples is to proclaim the forgiveness of sins in His name. This means that eternal life is not the old, guilty, frustrated life, but the forgiven and fulfilled life. This is what Paul meant when he said, "I am crucified with Christ: nevertheless I live; yet not I, but Christ liveth in me. . . . That I may know him, and the power of his resurrection, and the fellowship of his sufferings, being made conformable unto his death; If by any means I might attain unto the resurrection of the dead."

Christians do not survive death; they are raised from the dead.

Inquiring Layman: Surely a great many people would be astounded to hear what you have just said. I have always supposed, and I think that most people agree, that the Church teaches all Christians to believe in the doctrine of the immortality of the soul.

Parish Priest: This is a very common assumption, but it is not true. The Christian Church has never affirmed or denied that doctrine. In fact, I think it is a very inadequate and misleading doctrine. I do not think there is any part of us which can turn and say to God, "I am immortal. I possess eternal life. You cannot destroy me." Nor do I think that the doctrine of the immortality of the soul squares very well many facts, such as those that science has revealed. How can the soul be separated from the body? We know how much the mind affects the body and how the body affects the mind. How can we even think of a soul apart from a body?

Christianity affirms something very different from the immortality of the soul. We believe in the resurrection of the body. We believe that when a man dies, he dies completely. The whole man dies, and then God raises him up, giving him a new life and a new body.

Inquiring Layman: Now this confuses me. You say that we die and are to be raised up. When are we to be raised up, immediately after we die or will there be some day in the future, as our forefathers used to believe, when the trumpet will sound and the dead will be raised up? I have always thought it a rather ridiculous notion. Just imagine all those graves opening!

Parish Priest: In fact, quite a number of artists have tried to imagine it, but I agree that their attempt to do so has not been very successful. Obviously, we are dealing with matters beyond our experience and comprehension. Even the Bible gives no clear or decided answer. These things are shrouded in mystery and it is not the Bible's way to unshroud them. We find both the ideas you mention in Scripture. There are passages which seem to imply that the resurrection will not take place until the end of time when all will be raised at once and in the meantime the dead are asleep. Paul speaks of them as "fallen asleep in Christ". We may perhaps ask the question, does Paul mean by "fallen asleep in Christ" quite the same thing as merely being asleep and unconscious? Surely it is more likely he means that we are waiting with Christ and in Christ for His second coming in triumph.

Other passages suggest something rather different.

For example, in the parable of the rich man and Lazarus, Abraham and the rich man's brothers are all very much awake and show no signs of sleeping in spite of the fact that the final judgment has not yet come. Moses and Elijah both appear side by side with Jesus at the time of His transfiguration on the mount. On the Cross our Lord promises that the dying thief shall join Him in paradise that very day. And in writing to the Phillipians, Paul speaks of his desire to "depart and to be with Christ".

So far as the beliefs of the earliest Christians immediately after the New Testament times are concerned, it is certainly true that they prayed for the dead and it is at least probable that they believed the departed were still aware of those they had left behind. All through the history of the Church we find the conviction that the worship which we offer to God here on earth is in some way at one with the worship which is offered to God by the departed. This conviction finds its way even into our own Prayer Book.

Again, we would stress that all this language is poetry and point to the fact that these questions involve the relation of time and eternity so that we cannot possibly answer them in precise language. My own belief is that the departed share already in the resurrection, although the risen life in all its fullness cannot come until we can share it together.

Inquiring Layman: But what will be the conditions

of that risen life? What do you mean precisely by a new body? Will it be anything like the body we have here?

Parish Priest: Obviously, it is not the same body which was buried in the ground, but just as our bodies on earth are incarnate and express our total personalities, so in life beyond death we shall be given some instrument, some body in and through which our whole selves may be expressed.

Of course, we are in no position to know the details, but we believe it will be a richer, fuller life than this, one in which our individual selves will be fulfilled in God rather than destroyed. Such a belief transforms death from an enemy to be feared into a friend to be welcomed in faith.

A hospital chaplain tells of a woman who came in as a patient, facing a critical operation. She was tense, nervous, eager to have the surgery over. Also, she was a woman of great faith. At the time of the operation, the doctors realized that her case was beyond earthly hope. A few days later they told her the facts. Shortly afterward the chaplain went in to see her and found her sister in the room with her. The patient was relaxed and cheerful. She said, "Everything is fine, isn't it?" The chaplain wondered if the patient had actually been told the truth. At that moment, apparently sensing his confusion, the sister said, "Yes, all is fine for her, but not for us." You see, her faith had transformed death from an enemy to be feared to a friend to be accepted. She knew that, "If we live, we live to the Lord, and if we die, we die to the Lord." And that, "Whether we live or whether we die, we are the Lord's."

3 HEAVEN AND HELL

3

Heaven and Hell

Parish Priest: We were saying the last time we talked together that eternal life means essentially life with God, life in and with the eternal reality, and that the fullness of eternal life means an existence in which we are so caught up into the life of that eternal reality that nothing remains or survives which can divide us or separate us from Him. This is the real meaning of eternal life. And this is essentially eternal life for the whole personality of man. This is what we really mean by heaven; not a place, but a certain degree, intensity, and quality of relationship with God. Heaven is a name which we use to describe the complete and utter fulfillment of the whole purpose of man's life in the vision of God.

Inquiring Layman: That is an interesting definition

and, as far as I am concerned, a rather acceptable one, but I doubt very much whether it corresponds at all with the conventional Christian idea of heaven. What bothers me, really, is the way heaven is described in the Bible and other Christian literature. We are given pictures of the great white throne and a Lamb in the midst of it and beasts surrounding it; one has a face like a lion, another like a calf, and another resembles an eagle. They are full of eyes in front and behind. Fantastic! It reminds me of George Orwell's awful world of 1984 with its caption, "Big Brother is Watching You". You remember the passage. Big Brother was always watching from the omnipresent television screen. It looks as if those beasts are always watching everything that goes on in heaven. It is dreadful. Everyone wears white robes that have been washed in the blood of the Lamb and spends his time singing and playing a harp. The descriptions of the heavenly city suggest an ostentatious display of wealth. The foundations are adorned with jewels, there are twelve gates, and each gate is made of a single pearl. The streets of the city are of pure gold, transparent as glass. Who wants to live in a place like that?

Nor is this description confined to the Bible. Think of the hymns we sing about heaven, for example, such well-known and well-loved hymns as:

> Jerusalem the golden
> With milk and honey blest . . .
>
> or

And they who with their Leader
Have conquered in the fight,
For ever and for ever
Are clad in robes of white.

Can you imagine a man who has built a great industry by his thought and work and skill being content to live under such conditions? Would the statesman who has directed the course of history, or the soldier who has bravely fought in battle, or the pilot who has had the thrill of racing his plane at twice the speed of sound, or the mother who has brought up a family of active children—would any of these people be content with an eternity of hymns and harps? Is it not true to say that most people must find this idea of heaven undesirable and unattractive?

Parish Priest: Well, let's take your last point first. It is certainly true that those of us who have been in any life situation in which we have been of pre-eminent importance, and most of us in some situation in life feel very important in relation to other people, must all prepare ourselves to receive one great shock and that is that in heaven none of us can conceivably be important. There is still extant an old Latin rite for the burial of an Austrian emperor. Such personages were buried in a great monastic church. People carried the corpse of the emperor to the door of the church, and the door of the church was locked. They would strike on the door and say, "Open." The abbot inside would say, "Who is there?" They would reply, "It is the Emperor Karl, King of this place, King of that place," and so on. And they would enumerate all his titles. The answer would be, "We know no such person here."

Then they would strike again on the door, and the abbot from within would say, "Who is there?" They would answer, more simply, "It is the Emperor Karl." The abbot would reply, "We know no such person here."

Then they would strike the third time, and the abbot would say, "Who is there?" They would reply, "It is Karl." Then the door would be opened and the coffin borne into the church for burial. The Emperor Karl had gone to a place where he could not take his empire; where the statesman cannot take his statesmanship; or the general his authority; or even the mother, accustomed to ruling her husband and children, the kind of importance that she had known on earth. We must remember that heaven marks not only the final purging but the final extinction of the last remnant of our egotism and self-importance.

But with regard to your other remarks, we must again remember, as we mentioned before in our conversations, that the Bible, particularly when it deals with subjects like these, uses the language of poetry. The Bible's references to heaven are always poetically expressed. Take, for example, the writer of the last book of the Bible—a book which you have parodied, I think, rather unfairly. He writes a poem about the life of heaven, and he imagines it in terms of worship, the worship not only of men but of all creation, for even the beasts are there. Worship means for him, of course, the worship that he, as an early Christian of Jewish origin, is familiar with on earth, the worship of the Temple at Jerusalem. And so he describes heaven in terms of the altars, the candles, the lamps, the bowls full of incense, and the saints in their vestments, all the glories of the worship of God, as he remembered them in the Temple at Jerusalem, long ago perhaps when he was a boy. By the time he came to write the Book of Revelation, he was an old man, and the Temple at Jerusalem lay in ruins. But for him, as probably for all early Christians, this represented the proper way to worship God in spirit and truth, quite literally in the beauty of holiness.

Modern writers have often exaggerated or mis-interpreted the supposed simplicity of early Christian worship. Insofar as their worship was simple, it was simple because it was the worship of a persecuted church and had to be simple. But the early Christians were not in the least like a modern Puritan sect. Their minds were steeped in the traditions of the Bible, and for them the stately ceremonial of the temple represented the ideal kind of worship, the kind of worship which in the Old Testament God Himself had commanded His people to offer. It is in acts of worship such as this that we can best and most imaginatively enter into and anticipate the meaning of heaven. The life of heaven is continuous with our worship of God on earth. This is life eternal, to know God, and to know Him is to worship Him, and to glorify Him, and to rejoice in Him. This is life eternal—worship. This is the way in which this early Christian poet, a kind of primitive Dante, endeavours to do justice to his tremendous theme.

Now, what is the essence of worship? Is it not simply this, that in worship, at its highest and truest and best, in the worship that most of all fills us with its own spirit and engulfs us in itself, the tension between our duty and our desire is done away? The conflict between our love of God and love of self disappears. It is in our worship that, above all, we begin to enjoy doing what we ought to do. Now that gives us just one clue to the meaning of heaven. In heaven the life of the creature is utterly reconciled to the will of the Creator, and so we can say that in heaven, at least and at last, our duty will coincide with our joy.

Inquiring Layman: Yes, I can understand the joy of eternal companionship with God and of serving God, but I think you left out something vital. It is all very well to talk about life with God, but what about life with each other? Certainly, human companionship is one of the most precious things in this world, probably the most precious. Why, John himself implies in one of his Epistles that our love for God is meaningless without our love for one another. Now, I wonder, what is the place of human love in heaven? What about those whom we have loved and lost? Our parents, to whom we owe so much, husbands, wives, and friends whose companionship was dearer than life itself? The children whose time with us was all too short. What chance is there that these associations will be continued or revived? Will we recognize each other in heaven?

Parish Priest: Yes, I think we must say that, too. Indeed, it is implicit in what I have said already. You notice that the kind of worship in terms of which the Bible poetically depicts the life of heaven is essentially congregational worship. Heaven is more than the fulfillment of the mystic's quest for private ecstacy. The saints are essentially together before the throne of the Lamb. Man's nature is a social nature, and therefore the perfection of man's nature, the final flowering of man's destiny, must also be the perfection of a social nature, the final flowering of a social destiny. In other words, the very perfection of human life must be the very perfection of human community. Man is not, in the last analysis, a solitary individual. Man is a person living in a common life which he shares with other persons. That is really true here on earth, but the perfect, complete realization of it is part of what we mean by heaven.

We must notice, if you will permit me to change

the subject, that the opposite of all these things is hell. Hell really means unfitness for heaven. Hell is the consequence of a way of life and a kind of self-training which utterly and radically unfits a man for such satisfactions as heaven provides, a way of life which so emphasizes a man's own individuality, so blinds him in the fog of self-love, that he is incapable either of the worship of God or of unselfish living in community with his fellow creatures. Hell is the opposite of heaven. It is the fruit of a human existence which has rejected God and the worship of God and society as a sphere of unselfish service. From such a life there comes a final and ultimate failure to attain the true destiny of human nature in heaven, and this final failure to attain our true destiny in heaven the Bible calls hell.

Inquiring Layman: Now you introduce a subject that is revolting and highly offensive to sensitive people. In fact, it is offensive to many Christians. You have explained the symbols of heaven, but I don't think any man can rationalize or defend the descriptions of hell to be found in the Bible and in Christian tradition. Why, just think of some of them —the lake of everlasting fire, the devil and his grim angels, the torments, the bitterness, the despair. Men, for example Dante, have freely given their imaginations to this diabolical doctrine and have divided hell into regions and circles, presuming to compartmentalize this terrible inferno of human misery. Not only have they painted pictures of ghastly flames but they have reveled in describing foul smells and bitter icy cold. Think of the damage that has been done by hell-fire sermons, of the neurotics such sermons have made, and of the neurotics who have made them, of the children whose trust in God has been warped and distorted. Not long ago, a noted evangelist closed a revival with a *verbatim* rendering of Jonathan Edward's famous sermon, "Sinners in the Hands of an Angry God".

And yet all of this has been done in the name of the God who is supposedly the Father of Jesus Christ; yes, of Jesus Christ, who taught love and mercy and forgiveness. I am reminded of the Scottish preacher's story of the damned souls in hell who called out to God, "Oh, Lord, we did not ken, we did not ken," and God in His infinite love and mercy, replied, "Well, ye ken now." Is not the traditional idea of hell utterly incompatible with any belief in the love of God?

Parish Priest: I think here we have to return again to what we have had to say several times before. The language and imagery used about hell in the Bible is as poetical as the language and imagery used about heaven, and that language must be received as poetry. I believe one of the great curses of modern preaching has been the way people have literalized the great poetical images, have preached them as though they were all literally true. We must see these great images as poetry. The fires of hell are essentially the fires of frustration that necessarily burn in the hearts of the frustrated. For example, there is the well-known passage from Paul, where he says that, although he does not very much care for marriage and is not attracted to it himself, he thinks it is all right for those who need it. "It is better", he says, "to marry than to burn." Now, it is astonishing how many people assume that he means "It is better to marry than to burn in Hell" in the popular sense of the word hell, whereas, in fact, he means that it is much better to marry than to burn with unnecessary frustrations. The fires of hell are thus a poetical image for frustration, and frustration is precisely the state which a man brings upon himself when he lives the kind of life which makes him a person who could not conceivably enter into the satisfaction of heaven. For heaven is essentially the destiny of those who love God enough to enjoy being with Him.

Heaven is essentially for those who love their fellow creatures sufficiently to enjoy the life of an utterly perfected community. Heaven is not for the egotists. They could not conceivably fit in. They indeed would not be happy there. Heaven is thus the fulfillment of the deepest potentialities of our nature. Hell is essentially a way of life that utterly frustrates them. Hell is not something thrust or imposed upon us by God. Hell is the necessary consequence of the way in which we have responded, or rather, failed to respond to the love of God. And so we must not interpret all this imagery in terms of mere punishment. Hell is not just a horrible fate imposed upon us by a vindictive God. It is the consequence of our own terrible abuse of our own freedom which makes us quite incapable of entering into the life of heaven.

Inquiring Layman: I grant that men can abuse their freedom and that they may refuse the love of God and bring disaster upon themselves, but I am still distressed by this thought of hell. Imagine going to heaven someday and knowing that somewhere there exists a whole realm of unrepentant, bitter, self-centered people. The thought of such a place confounds my imagination. How terrible to think that those lost people will live on, century after century, millenium after millenium, with curses on their lips and rebellious pain in their hearts, becoming more and more hardened in their separation from God, more and more separated from all recollection of what is good or true, separated from all beauty, all courage, all tenderness, and all love. And just suppose that it is you and I who are among the lost, that it is you and I who finally abuse our freedom to such an extent that we lose God? Shall we then be in hell forever as conscious individuals?

Parish Priest: Thank you, indeed, for the warning that it may very well be you and I, for I believe that as we think about these things, it is important that each of us bears such a possibility in mind.

Now, with regard to your question: will the lost be in the fires of hell for ever? Here, I think, we must suspend judgment. I cannot answer clearly, for the Bible does not answer. I think the imagery which the Bible uses is at least quite compatible with a doctrine of the total annihilation of those who have placed themselves in such a position that they could not conceivably be happy in heaven. The fires of Gehenna, to which Jesus pointed when he talked about the fires unquenchable, are the fires that burned in the refuse destructors outside the City of Jerusalem. Centuries before, human sacrifice had been offered in the Valley of Ge Hinnom, and the people had therefore put it to the lowest and most degraded use imaginable. So the filth and refuse of the city were taken there and burned, and the fires never went out because, day by day, they were refueled with more of the filth and refuse of the city. The point is that the fire about which our Lord speaks and to which He points is everlasting, not because it is fed with a kind of fuel which is never consumed, but because it is continually being refed with new fuel. It is, at all events, conceivable; I cannot say more than that —that the fires of hell utterly consume, in an act of divine mercy, the personalities that have so abused their freedom as to put themselves forever and utterly outside the sphere of the divine purpose in creating them. It may be that in hell the remnants of the personalities that have so perverted and destroyed themselves will, indeed, dissolve into a merciful nothingness.

Inquiring Layman: Your answer relieves me to a considerable extent. It suggests the difference between painlessly executing criminals and torturing them. But must we think there will be anyone who will finally and irrevocably reject God? Such a view seems to imply that God will finally fail with some of us, and that is hard for me to accept. Of course, I know we have our freedom. Even human parents must give their children much freedom, and yet these same parents feel they somehow fail as parents if their children turn out badly. They expect some disciplinary problems, some youthful defiance, some bad mistakes; but, in the end, they trust their children will grow to be responsible men and women, and when our children do not do that, we ask, "Where have we failed?" Likewise, the teacher knows that he must grant his pupils freedom to make mistakes, but when these pupils show obviously that they have learned nothing, then the teacher asks, "How did I fail?" When my friend misunderstands me and turns against me, I am inclined to say, "How am I to blame? How did I handle the situation unwisely or unfeelingly?" We wait and hope that somehow the friend will again understand us and that the bond of love and trust will be restored. Is it too much to hope that somehow God will succeed, in the end, with every human being? That Judas Iscariot will receive the pardon of his Lord? That the proudest and most wicked rebel who ever lived will humbly surrender to this love of Christ? Is it not possible that, in the end, all will be saved?

Parish Priest: I do not think that we can deny the possibility. I am sure, however, that we should do well not to count on it. Certainly, there seems to be a suggestion running through the New Testament, particularly in the words of Jesus, that the tragic possibility of eternal loss is very real, and that we must take the danger of eternal loss with radical seriousness. On the other hand, it has been said, and I think with truth, that although there may indeed be a hell, we have no right to believe that any particular person is in it. Possibly no one is there at all. Also, there may be—and the Church has usually taught this in one form or another—further stages, beyond the grave, of purging and purifying, in which the imperfections we carry, so to speak, out of this world with us when we die are gradually purged away, and we are prepared for the final perfection of the vision of God in the life of heaven. This is usually called purgatory, which simply means a place of purging or purification. Some people do not like the word, because it has been associated in the past with many misunderstandings and superstitions. Nevertheless, I know of no really satisfactory alternative. It seems obvious to me that if I were to die, say tomorrow or the next day or even today, I should be no more immediately ready for the final vision of God in heaven than I am now and that, therefore, if by the mercy of God I am to be saved, I stand in need of some further stages of purgation and growth. This is what has always been called purgatory, and I think we should not be frightened of the word because of the many mistakes which have historically been connected with it.

So, to sum up my answer at this point, it is perhaps just possible that all will indeed be saved. We may hope for it. We may pray for it. But this is certainly not a possibility upon which it would be safe for us to count to any extent at all.

Inquiring Layman: I see what you mean: that we cannot count on God's love overruling our rebellion. But I still find it very hard to believe that anyone can actually be so bad or do anything terrible enough to be sent to hell. Why, think of how human ustice has been tempered with mercy during the last century or so. It was not more than a hundred years ago that teen-age children were hanged for minor thefts. Our courts of justice have realized that harsh and cruel punishments are not only brutal but useless. Criminologists and other students of human behavior have shown that behind the most wicked and criminal actions lie causes for which the individual is by no means entirely responsible. We know to how great an extent evil behavior is caused by factors over which the individual has little or no control; such as, hereditary weaknesses, poor environment, unusually strong temptations. We also know how much good is found often in the most depraved characters. Does not God know all this? Can we imagine a sin so terrible or a human being so evil as to deserve hell?

Parish Priest: Most certainly we ought not to doubt the reality and power of the mercy of God. Surely His mercy is greater than man's mercy and His understanding more profound and complete. On the other hand, if it is true that God has made us responsible beings, that is, beings responsible to Him for the span of earthly life and the ultimate destiny which He has placed in our care, then surely we cannot expect God suddenly to forget all about the moral responsibility which He Himself conferred upon us and treat us as though we were pitiful little victims of circumstance who cannot properly be blamed for anything we do or for the consequences of what we have done. G. K. Chesterton once said that hell is God's great compliment to the reality of human freedom and the dignity of human personality. Even in the realm of ordinary human intercourse, few experiences are more unpleasant than that of being forgiven by someone who forgives not because he is merciful and loving but because he despises you. "I forgive you," he says in effect, "because such a poor little creature as you are would have been quite incapable of doing anything else except what you did." We may be thankful that divine forgiveness is not that kind of forgiveness. God above all knows that man is not a poor little creature but His child created in His image for an eternal destiny. God must insist on treating us as the responsible beings that He has made us.

On the other hand, I feel you have asked your question in a way that thrusts us right back into thinking of hell as a kind of punishment which God imposes upon us in His wrath. Hell is not primarily a terrible retribution thrust upon us from the outside on account of what we have done in the past. Hell is much more a matter of our having to be, perhaps for all eternity, what in fact through our way of life we have become. It is not thrust upon us from the outside of our lives. It grows up, so to speak, from the inside of our lives. Heaven is God's heaven, but each man's hell is his own, a thing of his own making, a punishment of his own devising, a destiny which is the inevitable consequence of the shape and direction which he has given to his own existence.

Thus, we see how fateful is the question, what kind of people are we in the process of becoming as a result of the way we are spending our lives here and now? Are we, through our worship, through our fellowship with other people, acquiring and building up the kind of disposition, the kind of personality, which would be capable of inhabiting God's heaven with real joy and satisfaction? There is only one way of preparing ourselves to meet our ultimate judgment and our ultimate destiny—that is, to accustom ourselves here and now to discover and share in the deep and profound satisfactions of worship and prayer and of unselfish participation in the corporate community life which we live on earth in cooperation with our fellow man.

4 KINGDOM COME

Kingdom Come

Parish Priest: We have been talking about man's final
end and his eternal destiny. The Christians of New
Testament times were so sure of Christ's coming, so
completely confident of His victory and of their share
in that victory, that they thought of His coming as
something that would occur not in the distant future
but very shortly. Even during the New Testament
period they increasingly realize that this was not the
essential point. They saw that in the Resurrection
and in the coming of the Holy Spirit, Christ had
already returned to reign as King, and that even
here and now the Christian may share in that final
end as his life is fulfilled in Christ. They also saw
that the Christian companionship with God is not
terminated by death but that God raises us to a new

life after death, a richer, fuller life than life here on earth, the life of the kingdom of heaven. Heaven is the place where God reigns. It is man's ultimate goal. Heaven is declared to be man's goal at our baptism, when the Church prays that we may be inheritors of God's eternal kingdom. When we are confirmed, the bishop blesses us with the words, "Defend, O Lord, this thy Child with thy heavenly grace . . . until he come unto thy everlasting kingdom."

Inquiring Layman: As I see it, the difficulty about all this, for a great many people, is that life is not simply a matter of our final destiny. The trouble about this far looking-forward to our ultimate destiny is that it makes the experiences through which we are living now seem, by comparison, rather unimportant and insignificant. I remember a story about the late Lord Halifax, who was a very devout churchman. He was the father of the war-time ambassador to this country. He was listening to Bishop Gore and Canon Scott Holland who were talking about social justice in Britain; of the great importance of establishing more social justice in Britain. Suddenly and with great irritation, Lord Halifax said, "I can't think how you can be so interested in what happens in a world which is bound to be burned up sooner or later." For him, all that mattered was eternal destiny, eternal life, the kingdom of God, heaven, what happens at the end, not what happens now. Now, no doubt, those things do matter. If they are real, of course they matter. But surely they cannot be the only things that matter, and part of the trouble of thinking so much about these things, and talking and preaching so much about them, is that they do have the strange effect of making everything else seem unimportant. And so I would like you to face this question fairly and squarely. Would you agree that all this talk about eternal life in God's everlasting Kingdom, makes this life that we are living here and now seem unimportant?

Parish Priest: How could it possibly do so? If heaven is your destination, how could any part of your journey there be unimportant? If we are eager for people to realize their eternal companionship with God, how can we be indifferent to anything that affects their lives or their characters on earth? One hundred years ago, pioneers were streaming west in search of California gold. In order to reach California, they were forced to endure the hardships and hazards of crossing the plains and the rugged mountains. Were they not interested in making that journey as safe and comfortable as possible? Of course they were. Roads were built, the Pony Express was created to carry the mail, towns and trading posts sprung up where wagons could be repaired and provisions secured. In fact, it was not until the far western part of the country became somewhat populated and settled that much of the region in between was developed to sustain trans-continental trade and to round out the growth of the nation. Yes, the very fact that people were concerned about reaching the Far West immensely hastened the development of the Middle West. In the same way, the very fact that this earth is a stage on our eternal pilgrimage gives life on this earth infinitely more significance than it could otherwise have.

Edna St. Vincent Millay once called this world "an inn on a thoroughfare". It is the inns on the through roads that are the best maintained. If I am driving to Boston, I want the roads there to be kept in good repair. If I care nothing about going to Boston, the roads that lead to it mean nothing to me. Roads that lead nowhere are seldom kept up. There are roads which once led to thriving communities, communities now shrunk to ghost towns, and these roads have become overgrown, rutted, and washed out. So life in this world becomes overgrown with evil, rutted with sin, washed out in calamity, if the goal of life is forgotten.

Paul put the matter a little differently when he said, "Our citizenship is in heaven." These words have been rendered "We are a colony of heaven." Now a colonist has a recognizable attitude toward the land in which he is living. He is not like the explorer and the trader who look upon a new land simply as a source of wealth and exploitation and never identify themselves with it. Nor, on the other hand, does the colonist go to a new territory and become so completely identified with the natives and their way of life that he loses his ties with the land of his birth and rearing. Instead, he seeks to establish in his new environment the best traditions of his native country; he seeks in a very large measure to re-create the way of life that he knew and cherished at home. Because the citizenship of the Christian is in heaven, he is always seeking to make this world more like heaven.

Well, now, I admit that some Christians have been absorbed, almost obsessed, with life beyond the grave so that they have failed to live as responsible members of the human community on earth. There have been, for example, those who sat on pillars in the desert, but that was never the way of most Christians. Even the Christians who most admired these world-renouncing ascetics did not feel called upon to imitate them. Most Christians have always tried, at least, to follow Christ both when He said, "Lay up for yourselves treasures in heaven", and when He bade us pray, "Thy Kingdom come . . . on earth. . . ." The history of Western Civilization, the only civilization which was born and grew up under the influence of the Christian tradition, shows clearly that concern for man's eternal destiny and God's heavenly kingdom goes hand in hand with concern for the kind of life man lives here and now, and a desire to bring something like God's kingdom here on earth.

Indeed, this concern has been abundantly demonstrated wherever the faith has spread and the Church has been planted. Very rarely have missionaries confined themselves to preaching the gospel. They have founded schools and hospitals and homes for children and for aged folk who otherwise would have been ignored and even left to die. Whether in medieval Europe, in colonial America, in nineteenth-century China or twentieth-century India or Japan the story is the same. The Christian faith has ministered to man's total condition both in this life and for the world to come.

Inquiring Layman: God's kingdom on earth! Now that sounds to me a much more interesting idea, and, after all, we all are very familiar with it because it appears in the Lord's Prayer. But I cannot help thinking as I look back over our previous discussions that remarkably little has been said about this particular subject. We have talked about heaven and hell and eternal life, and so on, but not about God's kingdom coming on earth. You have really not said very much about that, and by implication some of the things that you have said have seemed to suggest that God's kingdom can only come by some great act of God in an eternal world. I should like you to tell me if there is any real sense in which we can rightly talk about the kingdom of God coming here on earth?

Parish Priest: Yes, there are innumerable ways in

which we can say the kingdom of God is coming on earth, and to do it we need not deny the deadly strength of the powers of evil and the grim results of their work. We need not even deny that evil constantly grows worse, as long as we do not close our eyes to the evidence of the growth of the good and the abundant signs of God's rule among us. Wherever God's truth and love are being shown, there the kingdom of God is coming.

I mentioned before that, when Jesus was challenged about His healing of those who were believed to be possessed of evil spirits, He answered, very significantly, "If I with the finger of God cast out devils, no doubt the kingdom of God is come upon you."

The kingdom of God came when our Lord rose in power from the dead. The kingdom of God came when the Holy Spirit descended upon the Church. The kingdom came when in spite of indifference, ridicule, and persecution, the Church grew until it survived the Roman Empire that sought to destroy it. The kingdom came when that same Church gathered up the fragments of an ancient, broken civilization and created medieval Europe. The kingdom came when the Church was purified and the Gospel freed from compromising entanglements with a dying civilization at the Reformation. The kingdom came as missionaries spread the faith over the entire world. The nineteenth century was called the "great century" because it was the period of the greatest geographical spread of the faith, when the story of Christ was made known to more human beings than ever before in history. The kingdom continues to come in our own time, in the ecumenical movement, in which the sundered parts of the Church of Christ are learning their oneness in Him and traveling slowly but definitely along the road to the reunion of a divided Christendom. In the meantime the Church has borne valiant witness to her faith in the concentration camps and in the prisons of Hitler's Germany or behind the Iron Curtain of communist totalitarianism. The new churches of the Orient have produced their saints and martyrs. And if the nineteenth century was the great century of missionary advance, the twentieth is one of the greatest in theological understanding and insight, and in efforts to relate the Gospel to the problems confronting Christians in a semipagan society. G. K. Chesterton once said that Christianity has not survived for nineteen centuries; rather it has died and risen again, time after time, because it worships a Lord who knew the way out of the grave.

Yes, the kingdom of God comes wherever the gospel is preached and wherever Christians pray in faith. Wherever the Eucharist is celebrated, our Lord eats and drinks with us in the kingdom. Whenever men give of themselves to each other; whenever they forgive each other; whenever they love and accept each other, there the kingdom comes.

Nor is the kingdom of God confined to those who profess and call themselves Christians. The love of God has flooded over into the entire world. Even paganism has become more responsible for human welfare. It is significant that modern paganism is often called, and calls itself, humanism, because of its responsible concern for human welfare. There are many things in Western Civilization of which we are not proud, but who would deny that in many important respects it stands up favorably with any other civilization that has ever appeared on the earth? From the West has come the abolition of slavery, the protection of human rights, a belief in the dignity and worth of every man which is the basis of human freedom and liberty. Yes, despite all the evil in the world, we can see genuine evidence of the establishment and growth of God's kingdom on earth.

Inquiring Layman: Clearly, you have said many things with which I heartily agree. Now I want to ask another and I think a more searching question. Does the language in which you have made your answer really commend itself to modern men and women? Of course we are impressed with the extraordinary survival of the Church through the ages, despite the sins and imperfections of so very many Christians. Of course we are impressed with the great achievements of our own Western Civilization, despite its many and terrible faults, some of which, to be sure, are still with us. But do we all agree in using the kind of language which involves the idea of the kingdom of God in expressing this great achievement? We see evidence of the establishment and growth, you said, of God's kingdom on earth.

Now, what I am really asking is this: is "kingdom" the kind of word which commends itself to the minds of modern men and women? For most of us nowadays do not usually think in terms of being in a kingdom in which we are subjects, as people looked after by the ruler, the king. Normally, we think in terms of progress going along the lines of more and more complete independence for individual men and women. The New Testament and what you have said today seem, by contrast, reactionary. Your language seems to suggest not democratic independence but increasing dependence upon the King who reigns in His kingdom as Lord of His subjects. Now, I realize that this is the language of the Bible, but I ask you whether it can be the language of grown-up, progressive, modern men and women. Is this what they can really understand? Is this what they can genuinely and sincerely idealize? Is this what they can truly desire? And so I ask you: do modern men really desire, or need, for that matter, any king or any kind of kingdom?

Parish Priest: This is an interesting question, and it is especially interesting in a country which is a republic and which, on the surface, at any rate, has repudiated the whole idea of monarchy and kingship.

I say on the surface advisedly. What made millions of Americans sit glued to their television sets in June, 1953, while a young woman was crowned Queen of the land from which we had declared our independence? Why did two broadcasting companies vie with each other to race those films across the Atlantic? Was it just sentimentality? I doubt it. Did not the coronation speak to a deep need which all people possess? Why, for that matter, do thousands flock to Washington to see an inauguration? Neither the American nor the British people wish to be governed by a tyrant, allegedly ruling by divine right, but there is something within us that responds to a symbol of authority exercised not only by popular consent but also under the sovereignty of God. Does not this suggest that man wants and needs authority of the right kind?

Just as man is created to depend physically on food and oxygen and rest, so he is created spiritually to depend on leadership and authority. I am sure that for all their rebelliousness, children prefer a firm authority on which they may depend.

Now, how do you reconcile all of this with the freedom of growing, mature people? I think the answer is that we are meant to become increasingly independent of each other in order that we may become increasingly dependent upon God. We set men free from tyranny in order that they may obediently devote their freedom to the service of

God. God alone can rightfully claim the unqualified allegiance of man. No one else is good enough to do it. Democracy is necessary not because men are good or equally good, but because all men are equally sinners. Only when men have no true God to worship do they fall down and grovel before human tyrants. For centuries, Christians have prayed in the words of the Collect for Peace to God "whose service is perfect freedom". Only as a slave of God and as a citizen of His kingdom does man find his freedom and achieve his destiny.

Inquiring Layman: All this leads me to go back to the thought of the coming of God's kingdom on earth. If God's kingdom is what men really want and need—not merely to rescue them from tyranny but also to give them the true loyalty and true obedience to the God who alone is really worthy of loyalty and obedience—if that is true and if we can in some sense, as you have already said, really believe that something of God's kingdom is being built up here on earth, then instead of hoping for God's kingdom at the end of the world, or in some shadowy hereafter, do you not think that we might have reason—that we might be entitled—to hope that God's kingdom may come here on earth entirely, completely, and finally?

Parish Priest: No, I should say no, at least not in any commonly understood and accepted sense of the term. If, by the establishment of God's kingdom, you mean a time when every man on this earth will have completely given up the self-centeredness which is his original sin and will have completely and unconditionally devoted himself to doing the will of God; if you, further, mean a time when every man will love his neighbor as much as he loves himself—then there is no reason to hope that God's kingdom will ever be completely established on earth. I hasten to add that such an opinion by no means implies that life on this earth may not be improved in many ways, that war, poverty, insanity, and disease may not be abolished; but I do not think that the time will ever come when there will be no tension between man's pride and God's will. I see no reason to believe that human nature will change in such a way that most people will cease to care more about themselves than about others or get much beyond the point of enlightened self-interest. Never in history will the Christian escape the painful necessity of choosing between evils. Never will he be entirely sure about his own motives. Never will he feel that he deserves well of God. Always he will know that he lives more by God's mercy than by his own virtue, and never will he mistake the most promising human achievements for the kingdom of God on earth.

But this does not mean that somehow God's will may be thwarted or that He will fail to establish His kingdom. God is capable of using even our sins and mistakes for His good purposes. Isaiah, the prophet, could point to the ruthless Assyrian Empire and call it "the rod of God's anger and the staff of his fury". God does not send evil into the world, but certainly He uses evil for final good. God's rule is shown on earth in the catastrophe and judgment that result from man's sinful defiance of God's love.

Inquiring Layman: Well, now, in answering that question you have thrown in, so to speak, a new idea which I find surprising and difficult. Instead of talking about God's kingdom coming on earth, you are talking about God's judgment showing itself on earth. I always thought that, in the Bible and in Christian teaching, the judgment of God was a last judgment which comes at the end of the world. I never supposed that we were to imagine that many of the catastrophies and misfortunes that we suffer here on earth are in time to be interpreted as representing the judgment of God. I should like clarification on this point. Are you really suggesting that in addition to the last judgment at the end of the world, there is also a judgment of God here and now on earth?

Parish Priest: Most assuredly I am! I have mentioned Isaiah. He and other prophets of the Old Testament were certain that God was constantly involved in human affairs, and that the fortunes of nations and the rise and fall of empires were evidence of the working out of His judgment. Man always has the choice either to conform to the will of God and to live by the law of God, or to defy that will and to be broken upon that law. It has been well said that if you jump out of the top floor of a high building, you do not break the law of gravity, you illustrate it. So you cannot break the law of God, you can only live by it or be crushed upon it. Those who will not know God as love must know Him as wrath. This is the judgment. This is the eternal judgment of God in the lives of man, and the last judgment is simply the place where the results of our decisions are so fixed as to become final. For any individual man or woman, the last judgment is the place where he looks at God and says either, "Thy will be done", or "my will be done", and then takes the consequences. And one day, for the entire human race, will come this final judgment when all will understand God's will and see how they stand in relation to it.

The final test, the last judgment upon any man, is his response to Jesus Christ. "God sent not His Son into the world to condemn the world, but to save the world." And the world judged itself by its response. "And this is the judgment, that light is come into the world, and men loved darkness rather than light because their deeds were evil."

How fitting it is to talk about human destiny on the very threshold of Christmas! For Christmas means that God has given us the King. It means that God's nature and character are most truly shown, not in the power that creates the galaxies and moves the stars in their courses, but in a Child lying in a manger, and in a Man hanging on a cross, and in the Son of God risen from the dead. The Nativity was the beginning of a mighty deliverance, the gracious act of a Heavenly Father who will not leave men in their self-centered, hellish prisons, but who will come to earth and suffer to free them, who will send His Son to be born in poverty and to die in pain. "Thou shalt call his name Jesus, for he shall save his people from their sins."

For in Christ is revealed the fullness and the depth of the love God bears to the human beings that He has made. And in Christ is revealed the marvelous destiny God has prepared for those who accept His love, as well as the tragic judgment that inevitably befalls those who refuse it. God has sent the Revealer. The question is whether or not our philosophy of life will let him reveal anything to us.